Brigid Magick of the Goddess

S Rob

ISBN:1540591980
ISBN-13:9781540591982

DEDICATION

I dedicate this book to the Goddess Brigid.

CONTENTS

ACKNOWLEDGMENTS

The existence of magick in all its forms.

CHAPTER 1

The magick you will learn within this book uses the power of Brigid ancient goddess and of course the power that you have. You will focus your power by using the correct methods: those that are shown here: and in this way, you will learn that Brigid can help you have a better life and even change the fabric of reality. Brigid also known as Brigit, Brig, Bhrighde, Brighid, Bride, Brighid, Brid, Brigh, Breeshey, Ffraid, Brigantia, Brittania and even Brigandu, has a name which means fiery arrow or bright one; is a widely used Celtic goddess who was used originally in British Isles and Beyond and now her influence has spread even further. But as a goddess she stands out because of the various powers and abilities that she has: Brigid is a goddess of the spring, fertility, healing, poetry, inspiring metal making and using and other crafts, but also divination and is a goddess of protection. However, through Brigid being absorbed into Christianity and a Christian saint she is also linked to, the hearth, and fire, agriculture, abundance, has the power to communicate with all animals and has power over animal fertility. Brigid also has power over fire and water:

both ancient elements. She is also linked to the symbol of a white snake: especially a white snake curled around a wand.

You can see that Brigid is a powerful goddess: or saint: and that she has so many areas of power that it is easy to see why some people would consider her a goddess of everything, and this means that many people simply use her for anything they want. In fact, how she sees the world is defined by her areas of power and they are so wide that she will indeed see the world in a very full way. This means that she is very flexible how she sees things and you could use her in that way quite easily and nothing would be wrong with this. But we also know more about Brigid and this is that she was one of the Tuatha De Danann: the ancient kings and queens of Ireland and those that became the fairy folk when they lost their position as kings and queens. But more importantly they adapted and did not die. This does mean that Christianity has made a fairy into a saint: but if the Pope does not mind then neither should we. Her father is The Dagda, the father figure, chieftain and Druid of the Tuatha De Danann. But if this is not enough Brigid is not merely one but is also three. She is a triple goddess: three and also one or perhaps easier to think of as one goddess with three manifestations. She is therefore Brigid the poet, Brigid the healer and Brigid the blacksmith. But this simply groups her many power and abilities.

However, to use Brigid I will be showing to you first a simply way that is simply like a prayer and this means that they appear fully if they choose. This does mean that Brigid will not be summoned and made to appear but she will hear your words and so the magick will be done as you wish it to be. This does mean that you should say the words of this prayer that I show to you now aloud while truly wanting them to work. This first magick however is for protection and it will protect you from the various attacks and maladies that can affect us: including curses and hexes.

Protected by Brigid

Grant Brigid, Grant Brigit, Grant Brig, Grant Bhrighde, Grant Brighid, Grant Bride, Grant Brighid, Grant Brid, Grant Brigh, Grant Breeshey, Grant Ffraid, Grant Brigantia, Grant Brittania, Grant Brigandu: the three that is one: protection. Brigid goddess of fertility, healing, poetry, metal craft, goddess of fire and water, solar goddess, she that was named a Saint, she with the power of divination, protection, she that can talk to the animals, she with the power of abundance and over agriculture I ask that you protect me. Brigid, of the Tuatha De Dannan that were the ancient Kings and Queens old ancient Ireland, those from who the fairies sprang, she with powers wide ranging I ask that you protect me from all attacks of all kinds whether magical or not, whether from humans or entities of any kind and this is what I ask of you. Brigid the goddess agrees to help. So it is and will be.

As I am sure you can see the magick you have learned is easy and yet still very powerful. This magick will protect you and will make your life easier. But the way of protective magick is that we see its effect, because we do not see the things that did not happen to us. But this does not mean it is not important in fact I would say that protective magick is of great importance to us. With this in mind I will now show to you protective magick that uses the power of Brigid but this magick will also use the power of Hermes. In fact, Hermes is a Greek god that among other powers, has the ability to thin borders: this means that he can thin the border between this realm and the realm of the Tuatha De Danann and so help you summon Brigid so that she can be seen by you, or at least her presence felt. This means that Hermes will be used at the start and the end of the ritual that follows: this is because it will enable you to thicken the border which is opened: this is always good practice. This magick is again for you to gain protection but this time the protection will be stronger.

Summoning ritual to be protected by Brigid

Hermes powerful Greek god of ancient times, you are powerful and have power over travel, thieves, sports, athletes, you are a guide to the underworld, and all borders are yours to control. Hermes, I ask that you thin the border so that the land of the Tuatha De Dannan is right here beside me now. Hermes thin the border, thin the border more. Hermes thins the border: the border is gone. I call Brigid great Goddess she also named, Brigid, Brigit, Brig, Bhrighde, Brighid, Bride, Brighid, Brid, Brigh, Breeshey, Ffraid, Brigantia, Brittania, Brigandu: the three that is one, through the border to this world. Brigid the great Goddess she also named, Brigid, Brigit, Brig, Bhrighde, Brighid, Bride, Brighid, Brid, Brigh, Breeshey, Ffraid, Brigantia, Brittania, Brigandu steps through the border and is here with me. Brigid goddess of fertility, healing, poetry, metal craft, goddess of fire and water, solar goddess, she that was named a Saint, she with the power of divination, protection, she that can talk to the animals, she with the power of abundance and over agriculture I ask that you help me. Brigid, of the Tuatha De Dannan that were the ancient Kings and Queens old ancient Ireland, those from who the fairies sprang, she with powers wide ranging I ask that you protect me from all attacks of all kinds whether magical or not, whether from humans or entities of any kind and this is what I ask of you. Brigid the goddess agrees to help and departs back through the border. Hermes powerful Greek god of ancient times, you are powerful and have power over travel, thieves, sports, athletes, you are a guide to the underworld, and all borders are yours to control. Hermes, I ask that you thicken the border so that the land of the Tuatha De Dannan is separated again from this land. Hermes thicken the border, thicken the border more. Hermes thickens the border: the border is back in place and solid. So it is and will be.

The magick you have learnt now gives to you protection: but because of this it also gives to you peace of mind. But when working this magick: especially the last of this chapter: you may well feel the presence of Brigid. It is also quite possible that you will feel her physically as a change in temperature and you may well even see her: although it is rarer. But you will know the power of Brigid because although this is protective magick it does help you to get used to feeling Brigid around you, and also helps you because she will have worked magick with you and so been introduced. In fact, the magick in this chapter will greatly facilitate all other magick with Brigid, and so it should be used be everyone. But it also is a good way of practicing magick because everyone can work protective magick whenever they want. It is the magick you can use to practice when you do not know what magick to perform.

CHAPTER 2

We all have problems and so I will show to you some magick that is to be healed. In fact, healing can be multifaceted, but first here is some magick for physical healing. The first magick is actually short and can be used if you have little time. When working this first magick you are praying to Brigid but it is unlikely you will see her: but she will help you. Just say these words that follow while wanting them to work and they will.

Prayer to Brigid for physical healing

Grant Brigid, Grant Brigit, Grant Brig, Grant Bhrighde, Grant Brighid, Grant Bride, Grant Brighid, Grant Brid, Grant Brigh, Grant Breeshey, Grant Ffraid, Grant Brigantia, Grant Brittania, Grant Brigandu: the three that is one: protection. Brigid goddess of fertility, healing, poetry, metal craft, goddess of fire and water, solar goddess, she that was named a Saint, she with the power of divination, protection, she that can talk to the animals, she with the power of abundance and over agriculture I ask that you heal my physically. Brigid, of the Tuatha De Dannan that were the ancient Kings and

Queens old ancient Ireland, those from who the fairies sprang, she with powers wide ranging I ask that you physically heal me so that I will be healed and be well and this is what I ask of you. Brigid the goddess agrees to help. So it is and will be.

I will now show to you a ritual that you can perform to be healed physically. This means that the healing you will get here will be of a body or physical nature. This does not fix psychological problems but it can heal the physical and this includes problems of the brain. But do not think that you must choose this magick or the last and I would recommend that everyone uses both because the power to heal frees us from many of life's problems. You are much more likely to see Brigid with this next ritual than the last prayer.

Ritual for Brigid to physically heal

Hermes powerful Greek god of ancient times, you are powerful and have power over travel, thieves, sports, athletes, you are a guide to the underworld, and all borders are yours to control. Hermes, I ask that you thin the border so that the land of the Tuatha De Dannan is right here beside me now. Hermes thin the border, thin the border more. Hermes thins the border: the border is gone. I call Brigid great Goddess she also named, Brigid, Brigit, Brig, Bhrighde, Brighid, Bride, Brighid, Brid, Brigh, Breeshey, Ffraid, Brigantia, Brittania, Brigandu: the three who is many, through the border to this world. Brigid the great Goddess she also named, Brigid, Brigit, Brig, Bhrighde, Brighid, Bride, Brighid, Brid, Brigh, Breeshey, Ffraid, Brigantia, Brittania, Brigandu steps through the border and is here with me. Brigid goddess of fertility, healing, poetry, metal craft, goddess of fire and water, solar goddess, she that was named a Saint, she with the power of divination, protection, she that can talk to the animals, she with the power of abundance and over agriculture I ask that you help me. Brigid, of the Tuatha De Dannan that were the ancient Kings and Queens old ancient Ireland, those from who the fairies sprang, she with powers wide ranging I ask that you physically heal me from all illness and physical problems and this is what I ask of you. Brigid the goddess agrees to help and departs back through the border. Hermes powerful Greek god of ancient times, you are powerful and have power over travel, thieves, sports, athletes, you are a guide to the underworld, and all borders are yours to control. Hermes, I ask that you thicken the border so that the land of the Tuatha De Dannan is separated again from this land. Hermes thicken the border, thicken the border more. Hermes thickens the border: the border is back in place and solid. So it is and will be.

Many of the problems that we have are not physical or just physical and are actually mental, psychological or even spiritual. In fact, the power that Brigid has to heal you expands past that of just physical healing and can even heal these difficult to define things. I am not saying that you should not receive any medical treatment but that this magick can be used alongside any treatment. In fact, I am a big fan of modern medicine but this does not mean that occultism cannot help or should not. I think that occultism should be normal practice when we get seriously ill. Therefore, here is a short prayer to be healed of all mental, psychological and spiritual problems.

Prayer for Brigid to heal all mental, psychological and spiritual problems

Grant Brigid, Grant Brigit, Grant Brig, Grant Bhrighde, Grant Brighid, Grant Bride, Grant Brighid, Grant Brid, Grant Brigh, Grant Breeshey, Grant Ffraid, Grant Brigantia, Grant Brittania, Grant Brigandu: the three that is one: protection. Brigid goddess of fertility, healing, poetry, metal craft, goddess of fire and water, solar goddess, she that was named a Saint, she with the power of divination, protection, she that can talk to the animals, she with the power of abundance and over agriculture I ask that you heal me of all mental, psychological and spiritual problems. Brigid, of the Tuatha De Dannan that were the ancient Kings and Queens old ancient Ireland, those from who the fairies sprang, she with powers wide ranging I ask that you heal me from all mental, psychological and spiritual problems of all kinds and this is what I ask of you. Brigid the goddess agrees to help. So it is and will be.

This next magick is a ritual that is to heal mental, spiritual and psychological problems. But do not think that you should choose just one and that if you used that last prayer that you should not use this ritual in fact you should use both. Don't choose which to do, do them both and get the strongest effect possible. It is after all here to help just like all of the other magick in this book.

Ritual to be healed of all mental, psychological and spiritual problem by Brigid

Hermes powerful Greek god of ancient times, you are powerful and have power over travel, thieves, sports, athletes, you are a guide to the underworld, and all borders are yours to control. Hermes, I ask that you thin the border so that the land of the Tuatha De Dannan is right here beside me now. Hermes thin the border, thin the border more. Hermes thins the border: the border is gone. I call Brigid great Goddess she also named, Brigid, Brigit, Brig, Bhrighde, Brighid, Bride, Brighid, Brid, Brigh, Breeshey, Ffraid, Brigantia, Brittania, Brigandu: the three who is many, through the border to this world. Brigid the great Goddess she also named, Brigid, Brigit, Brig, Bhrighde, Brighid, Bride, Brighid, Brid, Brigh, Breeshey, Ffraid, Brigantia, Brittania, Brigandu steps through the border and is here with me. Brigid goddess of fertility, healing, poetry, metal craft, goddess of fire and water, solar goddess, she that was named a Saint, she with the power of divination, protection, she that can talk to the animals, she with the power of abundance and over agriculture I ask that you help me. Brigid, of the Tuatha De Dannan that were the ancient Kings and Queens old ancient Ireland, those from who the fairies sprang, she with powers wide ranging I ask that you heal me of all mental, psychological and spiritual problems and this is what I ask of you. Brigid the goddess agrees to help and departs back through the border. Hermes powerful Greek god of ancient times, you are powerful and have power over travel, thieves, sports, athletes, you are a guide to the underworld, and all borders are yours to control. Hermes, I ask that you thicken the border so that the land of the Tuatha De Dannan is separated again from this land. Hermes thicken the border, thicken the border more. Hermes thickens the border: the border is back in place and solid. So it is and will be.

You now have powerful magick at your disposal. Magick is here to help us, but to do this you need to work the magick and this means actually saying the words and performing the rituals. But also, remember that your power is important because it is through this that all other magick can be performed. It is through your power that the powerful Goddess Brigid is commanded. This means that when you use your human power correctly it is more powerful than that of Brigid. But you must use it correctly and this is a matter of working to our powerful traits and using the weaker traits of Brigid to command her. For this reason, Brigid like many gods and goddesses can be better thought of as magical beings. But this is not to say that we are not magical but that our magick is different. But if we use it you help not just ourselves but all of humanity so that we may all rise to a higher level.

CHAPTER 3

I now show to you some magick that will allow you to know the future. Although you can use this magick alongside divination methods, if used alone it will help you to know the future because Brigid will send you a sign. This will be some atypical event: perhaps something such as an unusual cloud formation or some other chance event and this will tell you what will happen. This does mean that it is best to look out for these signs when you have worked this magick. This next prayer therefore will help to point the way to a better future.

Prayer for Brigid to let you know the future

Grant Brigid, Grant Brigit, Grant Brig, Grant Bhrighde, Grant Brighid, Grant Bride, Grant Brighid, Grant Brid, Grant Brigh, Grant Breeshey, Grant Ffraid, Grant Brigantia, Grant Brittania, Grant Brigandu: the three who is many: protection. Brigid goddess of fertility, healing, poetry, metal craft, goddess of fire and water, solar goddess, she that was named a Saint, she with the power of divination, protection, she that can talk to the animals, she with the power of abundance and over agriculture I ask that you give to me a sign so that I know what the future will be and so what I must do to get the best outcome. Brigid, of the Tuatha De Dannan that were the ancient Kings and Queens old ancient Ireland, those from who the fairies sprang, she with powers wide ranging I ask that you give me knowledge of the future and this is what I ask of you. Brigid the goddess agrees to help. So it is and will be.

Do not think that, that last prayer is all you can do to know the future because there is much, much more, including this next ritual. If you take my advice do not worry about whether to use this ritual or the last prayer but use both. You cannot use too much magick to know the future and the strength of Brigid will therefore allow you to steer yourself into the future you want. This magick does not show an immobile future but gives you, insight so you can change what you want to through your actions.

Ritual for Brigid to let you know the future

Hermes powerful Greek god of ancient times, you are powerful and have power over travel, thieves, sports, athletes, you are a guide to the underworld, and all borders are yours to control. Hermes, I ask that you thin the border so that the land of the Tuatha De Dannan is right here beside me now. Hermes thin the border, thin the border more. Hermes thins the border: the border is gone. I call Brigid great Goddess she also named, Brigid, Brigit, Brig, Bhrighde, Brighid, Bride, Brighid, Brid, Brigh, Breeshey, Ffraid, Brigantia, Brittania,

Brigandu: the three who is many, through the border to this world. Brigid the great Goddess she also named, Brigid, Brigit, Brig, Bhrighde, Brighid, Bride, Brighid, Brid, Brigh, Breeshey, Ffraid, Brigantia, Brittania, Brigandu steps through the border and is here with me. Brigid goddess of fertility, healing, poetry, metal craft, goddess of fire and water, solar goddess, she that was named a Saint, she with the power of divination, protection, she that can talk to the animals, she with the power of abundance and over agriculture I ask that you help me. Brigid, of the Tuatha De Dannan that were the ancient Kings and Queens old ancient Ireland, those from who the fairies sprang, she with powers wide ranging I ask that you give me knowledge of the future so that I will know what I should do and this is what I ask of you. Brigid the goddess agrees to help and departs back through the border. Hermes powerful Greek god of ancient times, you are powerful and have power over travel, thieves, sports, athletes, you are a guide to the underworld, and all borders are yours to control. Hermes, I ask that you thicken the border so that the land of the Tuatha De Dannan is separated again from this land. Hermes thicken the border, thicken the border more. Hermes thickens the border: the border is back in place and solid. So it is and will be.

Although many people want to know the future, we should not forget that the past can also be a mystery. There are many things about the past that we do not know: even about our own. Memories are not perfect but with this magick the secrets that the past hold will be known to you. This may occur as someone simply telling you something you did not know, or as a sign that somehow reveals hidden past knowledge. For some people the past comes to them as memories. Therefore, use this next prayer and the past will be yours to know.

Prayer for Brigid to give you knowledge of the past

Grant Brigid, Grant Brigit, Grant Brig, Grant Bhrighde, Grant Brighid, Grant Bride, Grant Brighid, Grant Brid, Grant Brigh, Grant Breeshey, Grant Ffraid, Grant Brigantia, Grant Brittania, Grant Brigandu: the three who is many: protection. Brigid goddess of fertility, healing, poetry, metal craft, goddess of fire and water, solar goddess, she that was named a Saint, she with the power of divination, protection, she that can talk to the animals, she with the power of abundance and over agriculture I ask that you give me knowledge of the past. Brigid, of the Tuatha De Dannan that were the ancient Kings and Queens old ancient Ireland, those from who the fairies sprang, she with powers wide ranging I ask that you let me know the past and this is what I ask of you. Brigid the goddess agrees to help. So it is and will be.

I now present a most powerful ritual that will reveal whatever knowledge you need or want to know about the past. But the thing about the past is that once known this knowledge cannot be unknown. But ignorance is usually not bliss and is simply causes many problems and so this ritual can help. If used alone it will reveal whatever is hidden about the past but if used with the other prayer it will reveal all that is hidden.

Ritual for Brigid to give you knowledge of the past

Hermes powerful Greek god of ancient times, you are powerful and have power over travel, thieves, sports, athletes, you are a guide to the underworld, and all borders are yours to control. Hermes, I ask that you thin the border so that the land of the Tuatha De Dannan is right here beside me now. Hermes thin the border, thin the border more. Hermes thins the border: the border is gone. I call Brigid great Goddess she also named, Brigid, Brigit, Brig, Bhrighde, Brighid, Bride, Brighid, Brid, Brigh, Breeshey, Ffraid, Brigantia, Brittania, Brigandu: the three who is many, through the border to this world. Brigid the great Goddess she also named, Brigid, Brigit, Brig, Bhrighde, Brighid, Bride, Brighid, Brid, Brigh, Breeshey, Ffraid, Brigantia, Brittania, Brigandu steps through the border and is here with me. Brigid goddess of fertility, healing, poetry, metal craft, goddess of fire and water, solar goddess, she that was named a Saint, she with the power of divination, protection, she that can talk to the animals, she with the power of abundance and over agriculture I ask that you help me. Brigid, of the Tuatha De Dannan that were the ancient Kings and Queens old ancient Ireland, those from who the fairies sprang, she with powers wide ranging I ask that you give to me knowledge of the past and this is what I ask of you. Brigid the goddess agrees to help and departs back through the border. Hermes powerful Greek god of ancient times, you are powerful and have power over travel, thieves, sports, athletes, you are a guide to the underworld, and all borders are yours to control. Hermes, I ask that you thicken the border so that the land of the Tuatha De Dannan is separated again from this land. Hermes thicken the border, thicken the border more. Hermes thickens the border: the border is back in place and solid. So it is and will be.

The magick you have been taught in this chapter reveals that most hidden of knowledge: the past and the future. It means that you can make better informed decisions and that you have more power over the present and the future. But it does not mean that Brigid controls your life, or even that you must follow anything which seems like advice. It means that you have more power, and not less. Brigid is simply helping you but what you do is ultimately down to you. It is magick therefore that empowers and informs and shows that the world is less humdrum that you thought it was.

CHAPTER 4

Knowledge of the past is so important to many people that I will now present to you some magick to know someone else's past. This magick therefore is for you to know the past of a chosen person. But this should be someone that you know well enough to know what they look like and their name. But if you have these and they fulfil these requirements then you can perform this next prayer; you will need to say their name in the prayer that follows

Prayer for Brigid to give you knowledge of the past of a chosen person

Grant Brigid, Grant Brigit, Grant Brig, Grant Bhrighde, Grant Brighid, Grant Bride, Grant Brighid, Grant Brid, Grant Brigh, Grant Breeshey, Grant Ffraid, Grant Brigantia, Grant Brittania, Grant Brigandu: the three who is many: protection. Brigid goddess of fertility, healing, poetry, metal craft, goddess of fire and water, solar goddess, she that was named a Saint, she with the power of divination, protection, she that can talk to the animals, she with the power of abundance and over agriculture I ask that you give me knowledge of the past of <u>state name of chosen person</u>. Brigid, of the Tuatha De Dannan that were the ancient Kings and Queens old ancient Ireland, those from who the fairies sprang, she with powers wide ranging I ask that you let me know the past of <u>state name of chosen person</u> and this is what I ask of you. Brigid the goddess agrees to help. So it is and will be.

I teach you now a ritual that is the most powerful that I know of, that will give you knowledge of a person's past. But now just anyone past, but a person of your choosing. This is a significant advantage in many of life's situations because people have things that they wish to hide from the world, but with that knowledge you have a substantial advantage over them. It will assist you in making decisions regarding this other person, and also even help them: it is much easier to help people that we have some understanding of.

Ritual for Brigid to give you knowledge of the past of a chosen person

Hermes powerful Greek god of ancient times, you are powerful and have power over travel, thieves, sports, athletes, you are a guide to the underworld, and all borders are yours to control. Hermes, I ask that you thin the border so that the land of the Tuatha De Dannan is right here beside me now. Hermes thin the border, thin the border more. Hermes thins the border: the border is gone. I call Brigid great Goddess she also named, Brigid, Brigit, Brig, Bhrighde, Brighid, Bride, Brighid, Brid, Brigh, Breeshey, Ffraid, Brigantia, Brittania,

Brigandu: the three who is many, through the border to this world. Brigid the great Goddess she also named, Brigid, Brigit, Brig, Bhrighde, Brighid, Bride, Brighid, Brid, Brigh, Breeshey, Ffraid, Brigantia, Brittania, Brigandu steps through the border and is here with me. Brigid goddess of fertility, healing, poetry, metal craft, goddess of fire and water, solar goddess, she that was named a Saint, she with the power of divination, protection, she that can talk to the animals, she with the power of abundance and over agriculture I ask that you help me. Brigid, of the Tuatha De Dannan that were the ancient Kings and Queens old ancient Ireland, those from who the fairies sprang, she with powers wide ranging I ask that you give to me knowledge of the past of state name of chosen person and this is what I ask of you. Brigid the goddess agrees to help and departs back through the border. Hermes powerful Greek god of ancient times, you are powerful and have power over travel, thieves, sports, athletes, you are a guide to the underworld, and all borders are yours to control. Hermes, I ask that you thicken the border so that the land of the Tuatha De Dannan is separated again from this land. Hermes thicken the border, thicken the border more. Hermes thickens the border: the border is back in place and solid. So it is and will be.

Knowing someone else's future can give us greater knowledge of our own. It can also help us to understand what we should do in matter that relate to them and us. But it also has the power to let us know how to help them, how to be there for them. It can also be used to enable us to deal with opponents and enemies easily because knowing their future is knowing what we should do if up against them. Therefore, perform this next prayer and gain its many advantages.

Prayer for Brigid to give you knowledge of the future of a chosen person

Grant Brigid, Grant Brigit, Grant Brig, Grant Bhrighde, Grant Brighid, Grant Bride, Grant Brighid, Grant Brid, Grant Brigh, Grant Breeshey, Grant Ffraid, Grant Brigantia, Grant Brittania, Grant Brigandu: the three who is many: protection. Brigid goddess of fertility, healing, poetry, metal craft, goddess of fire and water, solar goddess, she that was named a Saint, she with the power of divination, protection, she that can talk to the animals, she with the power of abundance and over agriculture I ask that you give me knowledge of the future of <u>state name of chosen person</u>. Brigid, of the Tuatha De Dannan that were the ancient Kings and Queens old ancient Ireland, those from who the fairies sprang, she with powers wide ranging I ask that you let me know the future of <u>state name of chosen person</u> that which lies before them and this is what I ask of you. Brigid the goddess agrees to help. So it is and will be.

Although this next ritual is for the same thing as that the last prayer was for, it is more powerful and I highly recommend that you use them both. They are both here to help you understand the future of anyone that is of your choosing. I recommend that you perform this ritual and the last prayer if you wish to fully understand someone's future. They can both be used together and are both effective but will strengthen the effect of the magick.

Ritual for Brigid to give you knowledge of the future of a chosen person

Hermes powerful Greek god of ancient times, you are powerful and have power over travel, thieves, sports, athletes, you are a guide to the underworld, and all borders are yours to control. Hermes, I ask that you thin the border so that the land of the Tuatha De Dannan is right here beside me now. Hermes thin the border, thin the border more. Hermes thins the border: the border is gone. I call Brigid great Goddess she also named, Brigid, Brigit, Brig, Bhrighde, Brighid, Bride, Brighid, Brid, Brigh, Breeshey, Ffraid, Brigantia, Brittania, Brigandu: the three who is many, through the border to this world. Brigid the great Goddess she also named, Brigid, Brigit, Brig, Bhrighde, Brighid, Bride, Brighid, Brid, Brigh, Breeshey, Ffraid, Brigantia, Brittania, Brigandu steps through the border and is here with me. Brigid goddess of fertility, healing, poetry, metal craft, goddess of fire and water, solar goddess, she that was named a Saint, she with the power of divination, protection, she that can talk to the animals, she with the power of abundance and over agriculture I ask that you help me. Brigid, of the Tuatha De Dannan that were the ancient Kings and Queens old ancient Ireland, those from who the fairies sprang, she with powers wide ranging I ask that you give to me knowledge of the future of state name of chosen person and this is what I ask of you. Brigid the goddess agrees to help and departs back through the border. Hermes powerful Greek god of ancient times, you are powerful and have power over travel, thieves, sports, athletes, you are a guide to the underworld, and all borders are yours to control. Hermes, I ask that you thicken the border so that the land of the Tuatha De Dannan is separated again from this land. Hermes thicken the border, thicken the border more. Hermes thickens the border: the border is back in place and solid. So it is and will be.

The magick here is potent and also useful. But it also shows the influence that magick can have over the life we have and the life of others. Magick is not some rare gift that only a few have, it is something that can be learned and has the power to change your life: transform it for the better. I am writing this book to boost your power just as the occult has boosted mine. In this way, we embrace a fuller view of the world and also that which allows us to gain a more powerful better life. Knowledge that other do not have is power and so here is that power: although together this knowledge can transform everyone and humanity could ascend to the next level of power: humanity perfected.

CHAPTER 5

The prayer you will learn next is for success: for you to be more successful. It is better to be successful than not to be, and many of us do not care about much else. This is not to say that some trade must be made and some other aspect of your life lost: just that this magick can help you gain success easier than it would otherwise be. This next prayer is also great if you have limited time because it takes so little of it.

Prayer to Brigid to be successful

Grant Brigid, Grant Brigit, Grant Brig, Grant Bhrighde, Grant Brighid, Grant Bride, Grant Brighid, Grant Brid, Grant Brigh, Grant Breeshey, Grant Ffraid, Grant Brigantia, Grant Brittania, Grant Brigandu: the three who is many: protection. Brigid goddess of fertility, healing, poetry, metal craft, goddess of fire and water, solar goddess, she that was named a Saint, she with the power of divination, protection, she that can talk to the animals, she with the power of abundance and over agriculture. Brigid, of the Tuatha De Dannan that were the ancient Kings and Queens old ancient Ireland, those from who the fairies sprang, she with powers wide ranging I ask that you give to me success in all ways so that I will be a success and this is what I ask of you. Brigid the goddess agrees to help. So it is and will be.

Here next is a ritual for success: this being a ritual is incredibly powerful and it is quite likely that you will see or feel the presence of Brigid herself when performing this magick. But I would recommend that everyone perform this ritual, and the last prayer because it is of use to us all. It will after all make all of our lives easier and better: being successful in our endeavours will be easier.

Ritual to Brigid for success

Hermes powerful Greek god of ancient times, you are powerful and have power over travel, thieves, sports, athletes, you are a guide to the underworld, and all borders are yours to control. Hermes, I ask that you thin the border so that the land of the Tuatha De Dannan is right here beside me now. Hermes thin the border, thin the border more. Hermes thins the border: the border is gone. I call Brigid great Goddess she also named, Brigid, Brigit, Brig, Bhrighde, Brighid, Bride, Brighid, Brid, Brigh, Breeshey, Ffraid, Brigantia, Brittania, Brigandu: the three who is many, through the border to this world. Brigid the great Goddess she also named, Brigid, Brigit, Brig, Bhrighde, Brighid, Bride, Brighid, Brid, Brigh, Breeshey, Ffraid, Brigantia, Brittania, Brigandu steps through the border and is here with me. Brigid goddess of fertility, healing, poetry, metal craft, goddess of fire and water, solar goddess, she that was named a Saint, she with the power of divination, protection, she that can talk to the animals, she with the power of abundance and over agriculture I ask that you help me. Brigid, of the Tuatha De Dannan that were the ancient Kings and Queens old ancient Ireland, those from who the fairies sprang, she with powers wide ranging I ask that you give to me success so that I will be a great success and this is what I ask of you. Brigid the goddess agrees to help and departs back through the border. Hermes powerful Greek god of ancient times, you are powerful and have power over travel, thieves, sports, athletes, you are a guide to the underworld, and all borders are yours to control. Hermes, I ask that you thicken the border so that the land of the Tuatha De Dannan is separated again from this land. Hermes thicken the border, thicken the border more. Hermes thickens the border: the border is back in place and solid. So it is and will be.

If you need a prayer to help you become more successful in something of your choosing I have it for you next. But do remember that in many ways the work that is done is for something specific and so you must choose for yourself what this is. This means that this magick will be focused on making you successful at something specific. But it is also true that you can always try to back away from the success that this magick attracts to you. However, if you try to do this you will find that, at that point it will be too late and so embrace what success this magick gives to you.

Prayer to Brigid to be successful at something of your choosing

Grant Brigid, Grant Brigit, Grant Brig, Grant Bhrighde, Grant Brighid, Grant Bride, Grant Brighid, Grant Brid, Grant Brigh, Grant Breeshey, Grant Ffraid, Grant Brigantia, Grant Brittania, Grant Brigandu: the three who is many: protection. Brigid goddess of fertility, healing, poetry, metal craft, goddess of fire and water, solar goddess, she that was named a Saint, she with the power of divination, protection, she that can talk to the animals, she with the power of abundance and over agriculture. Brigid, of the Tuatha De Dannan that were the ancient Kings and Queens old ancient Ireland, those from who the fairies sprang, she with powers wide ranging I ask that you make me successful at state what you want to be successful at and this is what I ask of you. Brigid the goddess agrees to help. So it is and will be.

What follows is a ritual that can perform to get success in some chosen area of your life. This magick can bring success to you and you can be as specific as you want as of the type of success that you desire and you will find that this magick will give this to you. Of course, this does not mean that you should not help yourself and make your own efforts to gain the success you want, but this magick will help you while you do this.

Ritual to Brigid for success in an area of your choosing

Hermes powerful Greek god of ancient times, you are powerful and have power over travel, thieves, sports, athletes, you are a guide to the underworld, and all borders are yours to control. Hermes, I ask

that you thin the border so that the land of the Tuatha De Dannan is right here beside me now. Hermes thin the border, thin the border more. Hermes thins the border: the border is gone. I call Brigid great Goddess she also named, Brigid, Brigit, Brig, Bhrighde, Brighid, Bride, Brighid, Brid, Brigh, Breeshey, Ffraid, Brigantia, Brittania, Brigandu: the three who is many, through the border to this world. Brigid the great Goddess she also named, Brigid, Brigit, Brig, Bhrighde, Brighid, Bride, Brighid, Brid, Brigh, Breeshey, Ffraid, Brigantia, Brittania, Brigandu steps through the border and is here with me. Brigid goddess of fertility, healing, poetry, metal craft, goddess of fire and water, solar goddess, she that was named a Saint, she with the power of divination, protection, she that can talk to the animals, she with the power of abundance and over agriculture I ask that you help me. Brigid, of the Tuatha De Dannan that were the ancient Kings and Queens old ancient Ireland, those from who the fairies sprang, she with powers wide ranging I ask that you make me successful at state what you want to be successful at and this is what I ask of you. Brigid the goddess agrees to help and departs back through the border. Hermes powerful Greek god of ancient times, you are powerful and have power over travel, thieves, sports, athletes, you are a guide to the underworld, and all borders are yours to control. Hermes, I ask that you thicken the border so that the land of the Tuatha De Dannan is separated again from this land. Hermes thicken the border, thicken the border more. Hermes thickens the border: the border is back in place and solid. So it is and will be.

The magick in this chapter has all been useful and I am certain that every reader will find a use for it. But the magick here also shows that the success that others have may not be all down to their worldly efforts. In this way, it is enlightening and perhaps gives many readers a feeling that they have now secrets of success: and this is true. But use the magick to get its effects and if you do your life will truly be transformed and made better. The world is after all now more open to your efforts than ever because of the magical knowledge you now hold.

CHAPTER 6

Most people want love but many find, that finding love is difficult and not at all easy. But magick can help and because of the vast powers of Brigid she can help. In fact, it is simply a matter of wording what you want correctly. This however is something you do not need to worry about because it is done for you. Therefore, perform this next prayer and have love.

Prayer to Brigid to attract love

Grant Brigid, Grant Brigit, Grant Brig, Grant Bhrighde, Grant Brighid, Grant Bride, Grant Brighid, Grant Brid, Grant Brigh, Grant Breeshey, Grant Ffraid, Grant Brigantia, Grant Brittania, Grant Brigandu: the three who is many: protection. Brigid goddess of fertility, healing, poetry, metal craft, goddess of fire and water, solar goddess, she that was named a Saint, she with the power of divination, protection, she that can talk to the animals, she with the power of abundance and over agriculture. Brigid, of the Tuatha De Dannan that were the ancient Kings and Queens old ancient Ireland, those from who the fairies sprang, she with powers wide ranging I ask that you attract love to me so that love shall be mine and this is what I ask of you. Brigid the goddess agrees to help. So it is and will be.

I will now present a ritual that can attract love: but it should be noted that the effect is stronger than the prayer you have just learned. This means that this ritual should only be used if you want the strongest of love to be yours. But for those that want even more they can themselves perform this next ritual and the prayer above: this will give the strongest effect possible.

Ritual to Brigid to attract love

Hermes powerful Greek god of ancient times, you are powerful and have power over travel, thieves, sports, athletes, you are a guide to the underworld, and all borders are yours to control. Hermes, I ask that you thin the border so that the land of the Tuatha De Dannan is right here beside me now. Hermes thin the border, thin the border more. Hermes thins the border: the border is gone. I call Brigid great Goddess she also named, Brigid, Brigit, Brig, Bhrighde, Brighid, Bride, Brighid, Brid, Brigh, Breeshey, Ffraid, Brigantia, Brittania, Brigandu: the three who is many, through the border to this world. Brigid the great Goddess she also named, Brigid, Brigit, Brig, Bhrighde, Brighid, Bride, Brighid, Brid, Brigh, Breeshey, Ffraid, Brigantia, Brittania, Brigandu steps through the border and is here with me. Brigid goddess of fertility, healing, poetry, metal craft, goddess of fire and water, solar goddess, she that was named a Saint, she with the power of divination, protection, she that can talk to the animals, she with the power of abundance and over agriculture I ask that you help me. Brigid, of the Tuatha De Dannan that were the ancient Kings and Queens old ancient Ireland, those from who the fairies sprang, she with powers wide ranging I ask that you attract love to me: love from people that I can love back and this is what I ask of you. Brigid the goddess agrees to help and departs back through the border. Hermes powerful Greek god of ancient times, you are powerful and have power over travel, thieves, sports, athletes, you are a guide to the underworld, and all borders are yours to control. Hermes, I ask that you thicken the border so that the land of the Tuatha De Dannan is separated again from this land. Hermes thicken the border, thicken the border more. Hermes thickens the border: the border is back in place and solid. So it is and will be.

Many people do not really want love instead they want passion and sex. But if what you want is sex then the magick for love will be of less use to you than that magick that follows. This is because the next magick is to attract sex from people that you will find attractive and being a prayer it is very easy and short and can be said even before you go out, or on the morning to help attract sex to you.

Prayer to Brigid to attract sex

Grant Brigid, Grant Brigit, Grant Brig, Grant Bhrighde, Grant Brighid, Grant Bride, Grant Brighid, Grant Brid, Grant Brigh, Grant Breeshey, Grant Ffraid, Grant Brigantia, Grant Brittania, Grant Brigandu: the three who is many: protection. Brigid goddess of fertility, healing, poetry, metal craft, goddess of fire and water, solar goddess, she that was named a Saint, she with the power of divination, protection, she that can talk to the animals, she with the power of abundance and over agriculture I ask for your help: I ask that you help me. Brigid, of the Tuatha De Dannan that were the ancient Kings and Queens old ancient Ireland, those from who the fairies sprang, she with powers wide ranging I ask that you attract sex to me from people that I will find attractive and this is what I ask of you. Brigid the goddess agrees to help. So it is and will be.

I will now teach you a wonderful ritual that is to attract sex to you. This ritual is so powerful that if you are going out night clubbing to find someone, this is the ritual to perform: and it is well worth spending the time performing it before you go out. So strong is its magick, that it will help you to get the sex you want. It will attract to you lots of attractive people: they will find you irresistible and this does mean that you will have to deal with many people desiring your body and if this feels too much for you then maybe something less powerful such as the last prayer would be more appropriate. But for that that really want to chance it you can perform both although in the strongest cases you may find that the effect of the magick means that you may even have trouble holding onto your clothes and those around you end up shedding theirs.

Ritual to Brigid to attract sex

Hermes powerful Greek god of ancient times, you are powerful and have power over travel, thieves, sports, athletes, you are a guide to the underworld, and all borders are yours to control. Hermes, I ask

that you thin the border so that the land of the Tuatha De Dannan is right here beside me now. Hermes thin the border, thin the border more. Hermes thins the border: the border is gone. I call Brigid great Goddess she also named, Brigid, Brigit, Brig, Bhrighde, Brighid, Bride, Brighid, Brid, Brigh, Breeshey, Ffraid, Brigantia, Brittania, Brigandu: the three who is many, through the border to this world. Brigid the great Goddess she also named, Brigid, Brigit, Brig, Bhrighde, Brighid, Bride, Brighid, Brid, Brigh, Breeshey, Ffraid, Brigantia, Brittania, Brigandu steps through the border and is here with me. Brigid goddess of fertility, healing, poetry, metal craft, goddess of fire and water, solar goddess, she that was named a Saint, she with the power of divination, protection, she that can talk to the animals, she with the power of abundance and over agriculture I ask that you help me. Brigid, of the Tuatha De Dannan that were the ancient Kings and Queens old ancient Ireland, those from who the fairies sprang, she with powers wide ranging I ask that you attract sex to me from people that I will find attractive and this is what I ask of you. Brigid the goddess agrees to help and departs back through the border. Hermes powerful Greek god of ancient times, you are powerful and have power over travel, thieves, sports, athletes, you are a guide to the underworld, and all borders are yours to control. Hermes, I ask that you thicken the border so that the land of the Tuatha De Dannan is separated again from this land. Hermes thicken the border, thicken the border more. Hermes thickens the border: the border is back in place and solid. So it is and will be.

The magick you have learnt in this chapter is powerful and in fact for some it may be so powerful that they feel they be better only performing some of it. But this is fine because not everyone has the same wants and needs in life. But it is here for when you do want it, and it also will provide the most powerful of proof in magick. But do not hold back from using it too much because like most magick it has a time when it can and should be used. This means that there will be a time when you will choose to say the words of these prayers and rituals aloud to shape your life and destiny and that of others: a time to use real magick.

CHAPTER 7

Many people believe that money is power, but this does not mean that acquiring it is easy. In fact, one of the problems with money is that everyone wants it. It also is true that having money and connections makes getting money and all wealth easier. This means that those born wealthy are more likely to get it greater wealth than those that start off without it. But I am here to add some fairness into society so use this magick and gain more money regardless of your background.

Prayer to Brigid to attract money

Grant Brigid, Grant Brigit, Grant Brig, Grant Bhrighde, Grant Brighid, Grant Bride, Grant Brighid, Grant Brid, Grant Brigh, Grant Breeshey, Grant Ffraid, Grant Brigantia, Grant Brittania, Grant Brigandu: the three who is many: protection. Brigid goddess of fertility, healing, poetry, metal craft, goddess of fire and water, solar goddess, she that was named a Saint, she with the power of divination, protection, she that can talk to the animals, she with the power of abundance and over agriculture. Brigid, of the Tuatha De Dannan that were the ancient Kings and Queens old ancient Ireland, those from who the fairies sprang, she with powers wide ranging I ask that you attract money to me and this is what I ask of you. Brigid the goddess agrees to help. So it is and will be.

Well as it seems impossible to have too much money what you should do is use both the prayer you have just learned and the ritual that follows. In fact, the ritual is stronger but it does not mean that you should not use any other efforts to make money, but simply that you should use this magick and make the best use of any money or opportunities to make money that it presents. Do not simply replace your usual efforts with occult ones: but instead add the power of magick to them. This way your efforts will mean more than they ever have before. With this in mind here is the ritual to attract money.

Ritual to Brigid to attract money

Hermes powerful Greek god of ancient times, you are powerful and have power over travel, thieves, sports, athletes, you are a guide to the underworld, and all borders are yours to control. Hermes, I ask that you thin the border so that the land of the Tuatha De Dannan is right here beside me now. Hermes thin the border, thin the border more. Hermes thins the border: the border is gone. I call Brigid great Goddess she also named, Brigid, Brigit, Brig, Bhrighde, Brighid, Bride, Brighid, Brid, Brigh, Breeshey, Ffraid, Brigantia, Brittania, Brigandu: the three who is many, through the border to this world. Brigid the great Goddess she also named, Brigid, Brigit, Brig, Bhrighde, Brighid, Bride, Brighid, Brid, Brigh, Breeshey, Ffraid, Brigantia, Brittania, Brigandu steps through the border and is here with me. Brigid goddess of fertility, healing, poetry, metal craft, goddess of fire and water, solar goddess, she that was named a Saint, she with the power of divination, protection, she that can talk to the animals, she with the power of abundance and over agriculture I ask that you help me. Brigid, of the Tuatha De Dannan that were the ancient Kings and Queens old ancient Ireland, those from who the fairies sprang, she with powers wide ranging I ask that you attract to me money so that I will be richer and this is what I ask of you. Brigid the goddess agrees to help and departs back through the border. Hermes powerful Greek god of ancient times, you are powerful and have power over travel, thieves, sports, athletes, you are a guide to the underworld, and all borders are yours to control. Hermes, I ask that you thicken the border so that the land of the Tuatha De Dannan is separated again from this land. Hermes thicken the border, thicken the border more. Hermes thickens the border: the border is back in place and solid. So it is and will be.

There is a difference between money and assets and many times assets are what people really want. In fact, there are many definitions of an asset but a good one is anything which owning, makes you richer. It can therefore be thought of as something which provides an income rather than something which is a cost or expense. To gain assets easier perform this prayer that follows and you will find they will flow to you easier.

Prayer to Brigid to gain assets

Grant Brigid, Grant Brigit, Grant Brig, Grant Bhrighde, Grant Brighid, Grant Bride, Grant Brighid, Grant Brid, Grant Brigh, Grant Breeshey, Grant Ffraid, Grant Brigantia, Grant Brittania, Grant Brigandu: the three who is many: protection. Brigid goddess of fertility, healing, poetry, metal craft, goddess of fire and water, solar goddess, she that was named a Saint, she with the power of divination, protection, she that can talk to the animals, she with the power of abundance and over agriculture I ask that you give me the help I request from you. Brigid, of the Tuatha De Dannan that were the ancient Kings and Queens old ancient Ireland, those from who the fairies sprang, she with powers wide ranging I ask that you make assets mine, so that I will be wealthy and this is what I ask of you. Brigid the goddess agrees to help. So it is and will be.

Here is a ritual to attract financial assets to you. This means that things that can be owned and will give you greater wealth will be yours. The ritual should therefore be performed as well as the prayer for assets by almost everyone. This is because generally people want more assets and greater wealth and this ritual can give this to them. But perform the ritual and do whatever else you wish to do to be richer and you will be.

Ritual to Brigid to gain assets

Hermes powerful Greek god of ancient times, you are powerful and have power over travel, thieves, sports, athletes, you are a guide to the underworld, and all borders are yours to control. Hermes, I ask

that you thin the border so that the land of the Tuatha De Dannan is right here beside me now. Hermes thin the border, thin the border more. Hermes thins the border: the border is gone. I call Brigid great Goddess she also named, Brigid, Brigit, Brig, Bhrighde, Brighid, Bride, Brighid, Brid, Brigh, Breeshey, Ffraid, Brigantia, Brittania, Brigandu: the three who is many, through the border to this world. Brigid the great Goddess she also named, Brigid, Brigit, Brig, Bhrighde, Brighid, Bride, Brighid, Brid, Brigh, Breeshey, Ffraid, Brigantia, Brittania, Brigandu steps through the border and is here with me. Brigid goddess of fertility, healing, poetry, metal craft, goddess of fire and water, solar goddess, she that was named a Saint, she with the power of divination, protection, she that can talk to the animals, she with the power of abundance and over agriculture I ask that you help me. Brigid, of the Tuatha De Dannan that were the ancient Kings and Queens old ancient Ireland, those from who the fairies sprang, she with powers wide ranging I ask that you make assets mine, so that they will make me richer perpetually and this is what I ask of you. Brigid the goddess agrees to help and departs back through the border. Hermes powerful Greek god of ancient times, you are powerful and have power over travel, thieves, sports, athletes, you are a guide to the underworld, and all borders are yours to control. Hermes, I ask that you thicken the border so that the land of the Tuatha De Dannan is separated again from this land. Hermes thicken the border, thicken the border more. Hermes thickens the border: the border is back in place and solid. So it is and will be.

Being richer is now easier than ever before. But you must use all of the will that you can muster in performing the magick here. Humanity has a great will and this should be used when performing magick so that you put as much power into it as you can. But I also feel that it's important that you know that through this magick that you know that it is real: magick is real. This does mean that many other things that were perhaps impossible to you: or you thought they were: now are not. This does mean that there are forces in the world that exist that you may not have known about. But also, it reveals that in the world at large much of what is represented as fact is merely some elaborate façade which is not there to enlighten but to fool. The truth is in the world but it is often hidden but I have not hidden the truth here at all, all is for you to see, learn and know.

CHAPTER 8

There are times when a more vicious and attacking form of magick is required and I present here a prayer which fits the purpose: it is to curse a chosen enemy or rival. But this magick is not to actually hurt them, but for you to be victorious over them so that success and victory will be yours and they will find that they will lose against you and this is a worse curse than many others because it attacks what they probably desire more than anything. But you should know the person that you want to target this magick at well enough to know their name and what they look like.

Prayer to Brigid to be victorious over a chosen enemy or rival

Grant Brigid, Grant Brigit, Grant Brig, Grant Bhrighde, Grant Brighid, Grant Bride, Grant Brighid, Grant Brid, Grant Brigh, Grant Breeshey, Grant Ffraid, Grant Brigantia, Grant Brittania, Grant Brigandu: the three who is many: protection. Brigid goddess of fertility, healing, poetry, metal craft, goddess of fire and water, solar goddess, she that was named a Saint, she with the power of divination, protection, she that can talk to the animals, she with the power of abundance and over agriculture. Brigid, of the Tuatha De Dannan that were the ancient Kings and Queens old ancient Ireland, those from who the fairies sprang, she with powers wide ranging I ask that you make me victorious over state name of enemy or rival and this is what I ask of you. Brigid the goddess agrees to help. So it is and will be.

This next ritual is for victory over a chosen enemy or rival. But just as before you will be saying the name of your chosen person within the ritual. But you can use both the prayer and this ritual and steal what victory or success your enemy or rival has. Do not hold back from using this magick because I understand that for many people victory has an aggressive edge to it. But this gives the ritual more power and so do perform this ritual if there is a rival or enemy in your life.

Ritual to Brigid to be victorious over a chosen enemy or rival

Hermes powerful Greek god of ancient times, you are powerful and have power over travel, thieves, sports, athletes, you are a guide to the underworld, and all borders are yours to control. Hermes, I ask that you thin the border so that the land of the Tuatha De Dannan is right here beside me now. Hermes thin the border, thin the border more. Hermes thins the border: the border is gone. I call Brigid great Goddess she also named, Brigid, Brigit, Brig, Bhrighde, Brighid, Bride, Brighid, Brid, Brigh, Breeshey, Ffraid, Brigantia, Brittania, Brigandu: the three who is many, through the border to this world.

Brigid the great Goddess she also named, Brigid, Brigit, Brig, Bhrighde, Brighid, Bride, Brighid, Brid, Brigh, Breeshey, Ffraid, Brigantia, Brittania, Brigandu steps through the border and is here with me. Brigid goddess of fertility, healing, poetry, metal craft, goddess of fire and water, solar goddess, she that was named a Saint, she with the power of divination, protection, she that can talk to the animals, she with the power of abundance and over agriculture. Brigid, of the Tuatha De Dannan that were the ancient Kings and Queens old ancient Ireland, those from who the fairies sprang, she with powers wide ranging I ask that you make victorious over <u>state name of enemy or rival</u> and this is what I ask of you. Brigid the goddess agrees to help and departs back through the border. Hermes powerful Greek god of ancient times, you are powerful and have power over travel, thieves, sports, athletes, you are a guide to the underworld, and all borders are yours to control. Hermes, I ask that you thicken the border so that the land of the Tuatha De Dannan is separated again from this land. Hermes thicken the border, thicken the border more. Hermes thickens the border: the border is back in place and solid. So it is and will be.

Much of life comes down to power and it is often the case that when people explain what they want that it could either be gotten through power or that it is itself power by some other name. You may wonder if you are the best person to have power but there are many worse people and they probably have it already. This means that by performing this prayer for power you are not just helping yourself but quite likely everyone else too.

Prayer to Brigid to be powerful

Grant Brigid, Grant Brigit, Grant Brig, Grant Bhrighde, Grant Brighid, Grant Bride, Grant Brighid, Grant Brid, Grant Brigh, Grant Breeshey, Grant Ffraid, Grant Brigantia, Grant Brittania, Grant Brigandu: the three who is many: protection. Brigid goddess of fertility, healing, poetry, metal craft, goddess of fire and water, solar goddess, she that was named a Saint, she with the power of divination, protection, she that can talk to the animals, she with the power of abundance and over agriculture. Brigid, of the Tuatha De Dannan that were the ancient Kings and Queens old ancient Ireland, those from who the fairies sprang, she with powers wide ranging I ask that you give to me power so that I will be powerful and this is what I ask of you. Brigid the goddess agrees to help. So it is and will be.

The ritual for power must be performed while really wanting to be powerful. This does mean that the doubt that some people have needs to be placed aside. In fact, you are perhaps more likely to make a better world than those that already have great power. So do us all a favour and perform the ritual: and if you feel you really want power then perform the prayer and the ritual. In fact, performing both is what I recommend and here is the ritual.

Ritual to Brigid for power

Hermes powerful Greek god of ancient times, you are powerful and have power over travel, thieves, sports, athletes, you are a guide to the underworld, and all borders are yours to control. Hermes, I ask

that you thin the border so that the land of the Tuatha De Dannan is right here beside me now. Hermes thin the border, thin the border more. Hermes thins the border: the border is gone. I call Brigid great Goddess she also named, Brigid, Brigit, Brig, Bhrighde, Brighid, Bride, Brighid, Brid, Brigh, Breeshey, Ffraid, Brigantia, Brittania, Brigandu: the three who is many, through the border to this world. Brigid the great Goddess she also named, Brigid, Brigit, Brig, Bhrighde, Brighid, Bride, Brighid, Brid, Brigh, Breeshey, Ffraid, Brigantia, Brittania, Brigandu steps through the border and is here with me. Brigid goddess of fertility, healing, poetry, metal craft, goddess of fire and water, solar goddess, she that was named a Saint, she with the power of divination, protection, she that can talk to the animals, she with the power of abundance and over agriculture I ask that you help me. Brigid, of the Tuatha De Dannan that were the ancient Kings and Queens old ancient Ireland, those from who the fairies sprang, she with powers wide ranging I ask that you give to me power so that I will be powerful in all ways and this is what I ask of you. Brigid the goddess agrees to help and departs back through the border. Hermes powerful Greek god of ancient times, you are powerful and have power over travel, thieves, sports, athletes, you are a guide to the underworld, and all borders are yours to control. Hermes, I ask that you thicken the border so that the land of the Tuatha De Dannan is separated again from this land. Hermes thicken the border, thicken the border more. Hermes thickens the border: the border is back in place and solid. So it is and will be.

Magick is real and this makes the knowledge here valuable. But it also bestows upon you a fuller picture of the world. This means that you will be able to see that there exist many possibilities and not simply the few that you may have thought about before. It could be said that your mind has been expanded but you have complete control over what you believe or do not. You also have complete control over your own actions and this is because it is easier and better to not attempt to control everything. This is why I write this book but know that you will ultimately use this magick as you wish to. I also know that this magick is compatible with all and every type of magick or belief and so I am quite happy that this magick will be used alongside other forms of occultism and with different beliefs and ideas. I have presented here knowledge and provided different experiences caused by the magick here. But what I have given to you are options that you otherwise would not have.

S Rob

Printed in Great Britain
by Amazon